Jelly Roll Biography

Quick facts about Jason Deford's Life and Career

Anne S. Oles

Copyright © 2024 by Anne S. Oles

All rights reserved. No portion of this work may be reproduced, stored in a retrieval system, or transmitted in any form or by any means, electronic, mechanical, photocopying, recording, or otherwise, without the prior written consent of the copyright owner. Unauthorized use, distribution, or reproduction is strictly prohibited and will be subject to legal action.

Table of contents

Introduction **4**
Chapter 1: Early Life **6**
    Birth and Family Background 6
    Childhood in Nashville, Tennessee 7
    First Exposure to Music 8
    Early Challenges 9
Chapter 2: Struggles with Addiction and Prison **10**
    Early Drug Use and Addiction 10
    Legal Troubles and Incarceration 11
    Life in Prison: Growth and Reflection 11
    How Prison Influenced His Music 12
Chapter 3: Rise to Fame **14**
    Jason DeFord's Rise to Fame 14
Chapter 4: Musical Career **16**
    Jason DeFord's Musical Career 16
Chapter 5: Personal Life **20**
    Family and Relationships 20
    Struggles with Mental Health and Sobriety 22
    Weight Loss and Health Journey: 24
    Impact of Personal Struggles on His Music 25
Chapter 6: Musical Style and Themes **28**
    Blend of Hip-Hop, Country, and Rock 28

    Key Themes: Addiction, Recovery, Resilience..29

    Cultural Influences and Southern Music..31

Chapter 7: Achievements..34

    Chart Success and Awards:..34

    Social Media and Streaming Milestones..36

Chapter 8: Philanthropy and Advocacy...40

    Mental Health Advocacy and Public Speaking...40

    Charity Work and Community Outreach...42

Chapter 9: Challenges and Controversies...44

    Legal Troubles:..44

    Criticisms and Industry Setbacks:..45

Chapter 10: Legacy and Future..48

    Influence on Music and Upcoming Projects..48

    Impact on Southern Hip-Hop and Country Rap......................................49

Chapter 11: Discography..52

    Albums, Mixtapes, and Key Singles...52

Chapter 12: Fan Base and Influence...58

    Interaction with Fans...58

    Influence on Emerging Artists..59

    Social Media Presence...60

Introduction

Jason DeFord, known as Jelly Roll, has made a name for himself in the music industry by blending different styles like country, rock, and hip-hop. This mix creates a unique sound that shows his wide range as an artist. He started with early mixtapes that helped him find his voice, leading to his big break with a major record label.

Jelly Roll has achieved important milestones in his career, including his first songs appearing on the Billboard charts, which helped him gain more fans. He has also worked with many well-known artists from different genres, proving he can bring people together through music. His talent has earned him several awards and nominations, recognizing his contributions to the music scene.

In his songs, Jelly Roll often talks about his struggles with addiction, finding redemption, and social issues that matter to him. This makes his music relatable and meaningful to many listeners. Fans love him for his honesty and vulnerability, which help create a strong connection with them.

Jelly Roll is making a significant impact on the music world by mixing genres and highlighting important social topics. His relationship with his fans is built on genuine interactions and storytelling, creating a supportive community. Right now, he is enjoying great success with new projects and tours that show his growth as an artist. As he continues to explore and push the limits of his music, Jelly Roll remains a vital voice in contemporary music, inspiring many with his journey and unique sound.

Chapter 1: Early Life

Birth and Family Background

Jason DeFord, known by his stage name Jelly Roll, was born on December 4, 1984, in Nashville, Tennessee. Nashville is widely known as the "Music City," filled with a rich musical history, especially in country music.

While specific details about Jason's parents' occupations are not widely shared, they played an essential role in shaping his early life. His family faced financial difficulties, and these hardships shaped his upbringing in significant ways. Jason has spoken about growing up in tough conditions, which influenced the person he would become. Although there is no detailed information about his siblings or exact family relationships, his family environment was critical in his early development.

Music seemed to always surround Jason, given that he grew up in Nashville. Even if there was no known direct musical background in his family, living in a city famous for music likely contributed to his eventual career. From an early age, Jason showed determination and creativity, traits that would later define him as Jelly Roll. Family struggles and dynamics, such as financial challenges and possibly a lack of stability, greatly shaped his early life. These experiences gave him resilience, which later became evident in his music.

Childhood in Nashville, Tennessee

Jason grew up in Antioch, a neighborhood in Nashville. During the late 1980s and 1990s, Antioch was a diverse area, but it was also known for its struggles with crime and poverty. The neighborhood's challenges influenced Jason's childhood and outlook on life.

Jason didn't excel in school; he had behavioral problems and wasn't interested in traditional academics. Instead, his creative and rebellious side stood out. His circle of friends, some of whom had a positive influence, while others led him into trouble, played a crucial role in shaping his youth. There were influential figures in his life, but not all were positive role models.

Living in Nashville, Jason was naturally exposed to a wide range of music genres. The city's rich musical heritage meant that he was surrounded by everything from country to hip-hop, and this inspired his eclectic taste in music. He held part-time jobs during his youth, but at the same time, he found himself getting into legal trouble. His early encounters with the law were a significant part of his story, reflecting the challenges of growing up in a tough environment.

Jason's life in Antioch contrasted with the broader musical culture of Nashville. While the city was filled with music and opportunity, Antioch was a rougher neighborhood, and this contrast would later shape the themes of his music. His struggles in school, combined with the challenges of growing up in a tough neighborhood, laid the groundwork for his raw and honest musical style.

First Exposure to Music

Jason's first experiences with music came from the diverse musical landscape of Nashville. Growing up, he was exposed to hip-hop, rock, and country music, all of which shaped his musical interests. Some of the earliest artists and songs that had a significant impact on him came from these genres, although specific influences are not always mentioned.

As a teenager, Jason started to experiment with music by writing lyrics and freestyling. His personal struggles and the world around him began to influence the themes in his lyrics. Nashville's diverse music scene exposed him to different styles, and he was naturally drawn to hip-hop and Southern rap subcultures.

He began to blend his experiences with the music he was listening to, and this led him to start creating his own music. Although there is no detailed account of his early performances or recordings, it is clear that Jason was developing his passion for music. Music became an outlet for him, and it was closely tied to his life experiences at the time, including the challenges he faced.

Early Challenges

Jason DeFord's youth was marked by significant challenges. He became involved with drugs at a young age, and this played a major role in his early struggles. His substance use led him into deeper trouble, and he began encountering the criminal justice system. He was arrested multiple times and spent time in juvenile detention, which became a defining part of his early life.

These experiences deeply influenced Jason's worldview and later musical themes. His music reflects the struggles he went through during this period, with raw, honest lyrics that come from a place of personal hardship. Despite these challenges, Jason had moments where he tried to overcome his difficulties, but he lacked consistent support. His behavior affected his family relationships and education, further complicating his path.

Street culture in Antioch played a big role in shaping Jason's identity. He had to navigate difficult circumstances, which influenced the person he would become. There were pivotal moments during this time, but rather than breaking him, these hardships made him stronger. As he continued to face these challenges, his interest in music grew, and it became an outlet for him to express his pain and experiences.

Chapter 2: Struggles with Addiction and Prison

Early Drug Use and Addiction

Jason DeFord's drug use began in his early teens and quickly escalated. He started with marijuana and alcohol before moving on to harder substances like cocaine and prescription pills. This progression mirrored the environment he grew up in, as the drug scene in Nashville was prevalent, particularly in the neighborhoods he frequented.

As his addiction worsened, it took a toll on his personal life. His relationships with family and friends became strained, and the chaos of his drug use made it difficult for him to maintain any sense of stability. His addiction also impacted his education and limited job prospects, trapping him in a cycle of substance abuse and poor decisions.

During this period, Jason made a few attempts at recovery, but without consistent support, sobriety was difficult to maintain. His struggles with addiction found their way into his music, where he expressed his pain, struggles, and the realities of his life. These themes became central to his early songwriting, giving his music a raw, authentic feel that resonated with listeners. The influence of Nashville's drug culture was apparent in both his lifestyle and his lyrics.

Legal Troubles and Incarceration

Jason's involvement with drugs and crime eventually led to several arrests. He was charged with drug-related offenses and theft, which resulted in prison time. Specific incidents, such as drug possession and other crimes, landed him in trouble with the law. Navigating the legal system proved difficult, as his criminal record grew, and the punishments became harsher.

He served time in various facilities for both juvenile and adult offenses, reflecting the severity of his legal issues. During this period, Jason faced intense emotions, from fear to regret, as he grappled with his situation. His incarceration became a turning point, forcing him to confront the consequences of his actions and begin rethinking his life.

Life in Prison: Growth and Reflection

Jason's time in prison offered him space for growth and self-reflection. His daily routine was structured by the restrictions of prison life, but he found ways to use this time constructively. He participated in educational and rehabilitative programs, which helped him develop new skills and a different perspective on life.

In prison, he formed relationships with fellow inmates and some staff members who became mentors. These connections were crucial in his transformation, giving him guidance and support during this challenging period. Jason also spent time reflecting on his past, understanding his mistakes, and beginning the process of personal growth.

He maintained contact with his family, though this was difficult. These relationships provided emotional support that helped him cope with the isolation of incarceration. Music became a significant outlet for Jason during his time in prison. He continued writing and honing his craft, using his experiences to fuel his lyrics. He also explored spiritual and philosophical ideas that influenced his thinking and gave him a sense of purpose.

How Prison Influenced His Music

Jason's prison experience had a profound effect on his music career. His time behind bars shaped the themes in his lyrics, focusing on struggle, redemption, and survival. His music became a blend of hip-hop, rock, and country, drawing from the diverse musical landscape he had grown up with and the hardships he faced in prison.

Many of his songs reference his time in prison, giving them an authenticity that resonated with his audience. His prison experiences provided him with a unique perspective on life and society, which he expressed in his lyrics. This authenticity became a key part of his musical persona, helping him build credibility with listeners who related to his struggles.

Music also served as a form of therapy and rehabilitation for Jason. It allowed him to express his emotions and find solace during his darkest moments. After his release, his time in prison became a major part of his story, helping him connect with fans who appreciated the realness and depth of his lyrics. His prison background also opened doors in the music industry, as his journey from incarceration to success became an inspiring narrative that helped define his career.

Chapter 3: Rise to Fame

Jason DeFord's Rise to Fame

1. Entry into the Music Industry

Jason DeFord's start in music wasn't easy. Raised in Nashville, Tennessee, he grew up surrounded by the city's musical energy. After facing personal challenges, including time in prison, Jason turned to music as a way to change his life. Without many connections, he started recording tracks and performing at small local events. His songs, full of raw emotion and real-life stories, caught the attention of listeners who connected with his struggles.

His early performances and recordings showed his strong will and passion for music. Even when facing challenges, Jason kept pushing forward, determined to make his mark in the industry. What set him apart was how real and heartfelt his lyrics were, something his fans appreciated.

2. Southern Hip Hop and Influences

Growing up in the South, Jason was influenced by Southern hip hop, a style known for its storytelling and deep beats. He looked up to artists like OutKast and Three 6 Mafia, who mixed real-life experiences with the Southern vibe. These artists helped shape his own music, which often told stories of struggle, family, and life in the South.

Nashville's music scene, with its mix of country, blues, and hip hop, gave Jason a wide range of influences. His music was a blend of the

Southern hip hop sound he loved and the experiences he lived through. His use of Southern slang and real-life stories made his music feel authentic.

3. Breakthrough Moments and Mixtapes

Jason's big break came from his hard work and dedication. His 2010 mixtape Therapeutic Music was a turning point, showing his ability to mix real emotions with strong beats. Fans loved the honesty in his songs, and he quickly gained attention.

Each mixtape he released, like Whiskey, Weed & Waffle House and Addiction Kills, helped him grow as an artist. His fans grew with each project, thanks to his relatable lyrics and evolving sound. Using social media and YouTube, he reached more people, sharing his music without the need for a big record label.

4. Notable Collaborations

Working with artists like Lil Wyte, Struggle Jennings, and Tech N9ne helped Jason expand his music and reach new fans. His collaboration with Lil Wyte on No Filter was praised for blending Wyte's Memphis rap with Jason's Southern style.

With Struggle Jennings, Jason found a partner who understood his life experiences. Their song "Fall in the Fall" showed how well they worked together, sharing stories of hardship and redemption. This partnership helped Jason connect with even more fans.

Jason's work with Tech N9ne, known for mixing different styles of music, pushed him to try new things.

Chapter 4: Musical Career

Jason DeFord's Musical Career

1. Evolution of His Sound

Jason DeFord, known as Jelly Roll, started his career rooted in rap and hip hop. His early music reflected the raw, gritty reality of his life, with influences from Southern hip hop artists like Three 6 Mafia. However, over time, his sound began to evolve, moving beyond traditional rap. A key moment in this transition was his increasing incorporation of country music elements. Growing up in Nashville, Jelly Roll was exposed to country music from an early age, and this influence eventually found its way into his work.

This blend of hip hop and country made him stand out. He began incorporating acoustic guitars, country-style storytelling, and themes of redemption and loss into his music. Songs like "Save Me" showcased his ability to fuse different genres seamlessly, allowing him to reach both rap and country audiences. Fan reactions have generally been positive, with many appreciating his honest lyrics and diverse sound. Critics have praised his genre-blending approach, noting how his music crosses boundaries in a way that feels natural.

Jelly Roll's unique sound comes from his willingness to experiment. He didn't limit himself to one genre, instead mixing hip hop beats with country melodies, rock elements, and personal storytelling. This genre-defying style has helped him carve out a distinct place in the music industry, appealing to a broad fanbase.

2. Notable Albums and Songs

Jelly Roll's music catalog is vast, but certain albums stand out for their impact and artistic growth.

The Big Sal Story (2012): One of his earlier albums, this project leaned heavily into his rap roots. It featured hard-hitting lyrics about his struggles with addiction, crime, and redemption. Songs like "Need Nobody" showed his ability to connect deeply with listeners who had lived through similar experiences. The album was well-received within the Southern hip hop scene.

Whiskey Sessions (2014): This EP marked a shift in Jelly Roll's style, as he began to experiment more with country and rock influences. The songs were more introspective, with a mix of rap verses and country-style choruses. Tracks like "Smoking Section" gained popularity for their raw emotion and genre crossover.

Addiction Kills (2017): This album was a pivotal moment in his career. It told the story of Jelly Roll's battle with addiction, with themes of pain, recovery, and hope. Songs like "Only" stood out for their vulnerability, blending acoustic guitars with rap verses. The album was a commercial success and introduced Jelly Roll to a wider audience.

A Beautiful Disaster (2020): This release solidified Jelly Roll's place as a genre-blending artist. The album featured rap, country, and rock elements, with tracks like "Creature" showcasing his ability to mix different styles. The album's mix of heavy beats and emotional storytelling resonated with fans and critics alike. It earned strong reviews for its production and emotional depth, showing how Jelly Roll had matured as an artist.

Ballads of the Broken (2021): This album marked Jelly Roll's full embrace of his country influences, with heartfelt ballads that focused on personal struggles and redemption. Songs like "Save Me" became anthems for those dealing with similar issues. The album received widespread acclaim, with many praising its raw honesty.

Throughout his career, Jelly Roll's ability to evolve while staying true to his experiences has been key to his success. His music continues to resonate with listeners, both within and outside the country and rap genres.

3. Major Tours and Performances

Live performances have played a big part in Jelly Roll's rise to fame. His early shows were small, intimate affairs, where fans could see his raw emotion up close. Over time, as his music evolved and his fan base grew, so did his live shows. His stage presence is marked by his ability to connect deeply with the audience, often sharing personal stories between songs.

Whiskey Sessions Tour (2015): This tour was one of his first major headlining runs, showcasing his mix of rap and country. The performances were energetic, with Jelly Roll alternating between high-energy rap tracks and slower, more emotional ballads. Fans appreciated the authenticity he brought to the stage.

Addiction Kills Tour (2018): As his music gained more attention, Jelly Roll's shows grew in scale. This tour was a turning point, featuring bigger venues and a more polished live experience. His performances of songs like "Only" were particularly memorable, as they showcased the vulnerability in his music.

Festival Appearances: Jelly Roll's festival performances, such as his set at Rolling Loud and Bonnaroo, helped him reach new audiences. These festivals, which feature a mix of genres, were the perfect platform for his diverse sound. His ability to blend hip hop and country elements helped him stand out, with many festival-goers walking away as new fans.

Tour reviews often highlight his emotional connection with the audience. Whether performing at festivals or headlining his own shows, Jelly Roll's ability to make each performance feel personal has been a major factor in his success. His live act has evolved with his sound, and as he continues to blend genres, his shows have become a unique experience that reflects his journey.

Chapter 5: Personal Life

Family and Relationships

Relationship with His Wife, Bunnie XO: Jason DeFord and Bunnie XO, whose real name is Bunnie DeFord, have built a strong relationship that is widely publicized and celebrated by their fans. They met in Las Vegas and quickly hit it off, embarking on a journey together filled with mutual love and support. Bunnie XO, a podcast host and social media influencer, has played a significant role in Jason's life, helping him during his rise to fame and standing by him through personal struggles. Their relationship is marked by openness, with both often speaking about their love and how they have supported each other's growth.

Fatherhood and His Approach to Parenting: Jason is also a dedicated father, having a daughter named Bailee Ann from a previous relationship. He has been open about the challenges of fatherhood, especially as he worked to overcome his past struggles with addiction and criminal history. Jason's approach to parenting is deeply influenced by his own difficult childhood and life experiences, which have shaped his desire to provide a better life for his children. He often talks about how being a father is one of the most important roles in his life, and he strives to set a positive example for his daughter.

Influence of Past Experiences on Family Dynamics: Jason's difficult past, including his time in jail and struggles with addiction, has deeply influenced his family dynamics. His journey to sobriety and self-improvement is reflected in how he now approaches relationships, valuing stability, loyalty, and love. He has worked hard to rebuild his life and create a strong foundation for his family, often crediting them with keeping him grounded. His past experiences have made him more empathetic and resilient, which translates into his family relationships.

Significant Friendships and Mentorships: Throughout his career, Jason has forged important friendships and mentorships in the music industry. These relationships have helped him navigate his career, offering support during challenging times. He has often mentioned the importance of surrounding himself with positive influences, both personally and professionally, to maintain his focus and growth.

Impact of Fame on Personal Relationships: Jason's rise to fame has come with challenges in maintaining his personal relationships. The demands of his music career, including tours and public appearances, have put pressure on his family life. However, Jason and Bunnie have worked together to keep their relationship strong. His open discussion of his personal struggles, particularly his journey to sobriety and mental health battles, has resonated with his fanbase and has helped him maintain authenticity in both his music and his relationships.

Challenges and Triumphs in Balancing Career and Relationships: Balancing a music career with family responsibilities has not been easy, but Jason has openly acknowledged these challenges. The couple has faced difficult periods, especially when it comes to maintaining a stable home life while juggling the pressures of fame. However, their commitment to each other and their family has helped them overcome these challenges, and Jason often talks about how his family's support has been instrumental in his success.

Struggles with Mental Health and Sobriety

Mental Health Issues: Jason has been candid about his struggles with mental health, including depression and anxiety. These issues stem from a combination of his difficult childhood, time spent in jail, and his battles with addiction. In interviews, he has spoken about the weight of these mental health challenges, particularly as he navigated the pressures of the music industry.

Maintaining Sobriety: Jason's history of addiction is a central theme in his life and music. After years of substance abuse, he decided to commit to sobriety, a journey that has been both difficult and rewarding. His approach includes staying connected with support systems, practicing self-care, and focusing on his music as an outlet for his emotions. Jason's transparency about his sobriety has inspired many fans who face similar struggles.

Managing Fame and Sobriety: The pressures of fame have added another layer of complexity to Jason's sobriety journey. Being constantly in the public eye, while managing the expectations of a successful music career, has required Jason to be disciplined and intentional about his mental and physical health. He often speaks about how important it is to stay connected to his roots and avoid temptations that could jeopardize his sobriety.

Relapses and Challenging Periods: Jason has not shied away from discussing difficult periods in his life, including relapses. He emphasizes that recovery is not a linear process, and there have been moments where the pressures of life have tested his commitment to sobriety. His openness about these challenges, however, has made his story even more relatable and inspirational to his audience.

Therapy, Support Groups, and Coping Mechanisms: Jason credits therapy and support groups as crucial components of his recovery process. He has also mentioned turning to music as a form of therapy, using songwriting to process his emotions. Along with professional help, he leans on his family, particularly his wife Bunnie, for support during tough times.

Using His Platform for Advocacy: Jason has used his platform to speak openly about mental health and addiction, hoping to raise awareness and break the stigma surrounding these issues. His personal experiences have made him an advocate for mental health and recovery, and he often encourages his fans to seek help if they're struggling. This advocacy work has resonated deeply with his fanbase, many of whom relate to his struggles.

Weight Loss and Health Journey:

Motivations for Weight Loss: Jason's weight loss journey began as part of his commitment to improving his overall health. The motivation came from his desire to live a healthier lifestyle, especially after years of struggling with addiction and mental health challenges. He has often talked about how his physical health was closely tied to his mental and emotional well-being.

Methods for Losing Weight: Jason employed a combination of diet changes and exercise routines to achieve his weight loss goals. He focused on sustainable lifestyle changes, including eating healthier, cutting out unhealthy habits, and incorporating regular physical activity into his routine.

Challenges During the Process: Like many, Jason faced challenges along the way, including balancing his weight loss journey with the demands of his career. However, he stayed committed to the process, recognizing that improving his physical health was an important part of his overall recovery.

Impact on Self-Image and Confidence: The physical transformation has boosted Jason's self-image and confidence. He has spoken about how losing weight has made him feel better physically and mentally, giving him more energy and focus in both his personal life and music career.

Changes in Lifestyle and Public Image: Jason's weight loss has led to changes in his lifestyle, including healthier eating habits and a more active routine. His public image has also evolved, with fans and the media noting his transformation. However, Jason emphasizes that his journey is about more than just appearance it's about living a healthier, more fulfilling life.

Advice to Fans: Jason frequently shares messages of inspiration with his fans, encouraging them to prioritize their health and well-being. He emphasizes that transformation is possible, no matter how challenging it may seem, and that persistence and self-love are key.

Impact of Personal Struggles on His Music

Reflections of Family Life in Lyrics: Jason's music often reflects his family life, particularly his role as a father. Songs like "Same A**hole" and "Save Me" touch on themes of redemption, personal growth, and his commitment to being a better person for his daughter. His lyrics are deeply personal, offering insights into how his family motivates him to keep going.

Mental Health and Sobriety in Songwriting: Jason's struggles with mental health and sobriety are a significant influence on his songwriting. His lyrics often tackle heavy themes like addiction, depression, and the journey to recovery. This raw honesty has connected him deeply with his fans, many of whom appreciate his vulnerability and openness about these struggles.

Impact of Weight Loss on Music and Stage Presence: Jason's weight loss has also influenced his music career, particularly his stage presence. He has spoken about having more energy and confidence on stage, which has allowed him to perform at a higher level. The physical transformation has been a symbol of his larger journey of self-improvement.

Songs Addressing Personal Struggles: Specific songs like "Save Me" and "Son of a Sinner" directly address Jason's personal struggles, particularly his battles with addiction and mental health. These tracks have become anthems for fans who relate to his story, and they showcase his ability to turn pain into powerful art.

Authenticity and Fan Connection: Jason's authenticity is a key part of his appeal. Fans are drawn to his raw, unfiltered approach to storytelling, as he speaks openly about the challenges he's faced. This connection has only deepened as fans see how his personal growth mirrors the evolution of his music.

Evolution of Music with Personal Growth: As Jason has grown personally, his music has evolved as well. His earlier work focused more on his rebellious, rough-around-the-edges persona, while his more recent music showcases a more introspective and thoughtful side. This evolution has allowed him to reach a broader audience, while still maintaining the authenticity that made him popular in the first place.

Shifts in Themes and Style: Significant life events, such as his commitment to sobriety and his focus on family, have influenced the themes and style of Jason's music. He has gradually moved from a purely rap-focused sound to a blend of country, rock, and rap, reflecting his multifaceted experiences and growth. This genre-blending approach has made his music more relatable to a wider audience while staying true to his roots.

Chapter 6: Musical Style and Themes

Blend of Hip-Hop, Country, and Rock

Integrating Different Genres: Jelly Roll mixes hip-hop, country, and rock in his music in a way that feels natural. He blends the storytelling and emotional lyrics of country music with the beats and rhythms of hip-hop. He also uses rock-style guitar riffs and drums to give his songs a harder, more energetic sound.

Songs That Show His Style: Some of his songs, like "Save Me" and "Son of a Sinner," show how he brings together these genres. In "Save Me," he sings with a country feel but also includes hip-hop beats, while "Son of a Sinner" has strong country influences with rock energy.

Background and Experiences: Jelly Roll's life growing up in Nashville plays a big role in his music. He was influenced by country music but also listened to hip-hop and rock. His personal struggles, such as addiction and overcoming hardships, are part of why his music combines different styles.

Evolution of His Blend: At the start of his career, Jelly Roll leaned more toward hip-hop, but over time, he began adding more country and rock to his sound. As his music evolved, he found new ways to bring these genres together in a way that feels authentic to him.

Reception in Different Communities: People from different music scenes appreciate Jelly Roll's mix of styles. Fans of country, hip-hop, and rock all find something to love in his music. While some traditional country fans might have been unsure at first, many now enjoy his unique sound.

Success and Appeal: Jelly Roll's ability to blend these genres has made him stand out. His songs reach a wider audience because they mix different styles, making his music relatable to many people. His honest lyrics about real-life struggles help him connect with listeners.

Comparisons to Other Artists: Like artists such as Kid Rock and Post Malone, Jelly Roll doesn't limit himself to one genre. He freely moves between styles, making him part of a group of musicians who break the rules and combine different types of music in creative ways.

Key Themes: Addiction, Recovery, Resilience

Lyrics About Addiction and Recovery: In many of Jelly Roll's songs, he sings about addiction and trying to recover from it. For example, in "Save Me," he talks about feeling trapped by addiction and wanting to change. His lyrics often speak about the pain of addiction, but also the hope for a better life.

Personal Experience in His Songs: Jelly Roll's own battles with addiction shape his music. He's been open about his past struggles with drugs and alcohol, and this honesty comes through in his songwriting. His music reflects his personal journey of recovery and the ups and downs that come with it.

Resilience and Triumph: Many of Jelly Roll's songs also talk about resilience and how he's kept going, even when things were tough. He sings about making it through difficult times and finding strength in his pain. This message of not giving up is a big part of what makes his music powerful.

How These Themes Connect With Fans: Because many people have dealt with addiction, recovery, or tough times, Jelly Roll's music resonates with his audience. His fans relate to his struggles and find comfort in his songs. His willingness to talk about real issues makes his music special to many listeners.

Changes in Addressing These Themes: Over the years, Jelly Roll has grown in how he talks about these themes. Early in his career, his music focused more on the pain and struggles, but now, he often includes messages of hope and healing. His songs have become more balanced between raw emotion and inspiration.

Balancing Honesty and Hope: Jelly Roll is known for being honest about his struggles, but he also tries to inspire hope in his listeners. He doesn't shy away from talking about dark times, but he always includes a message that things can get better, helping his fans feel encouraged.

Comparisons to Other Artists: Jelly Roll's approach to addiction and recovery is similar to artists like Eminem, who also sings about overcoming struggles with addiction. Both artists use their music to share their personal journeys and to inspire others who are going through tough times.

Cultural Influences and Southern Music

Nashville Roots in His Music: Growing up in Nashville, Jelly Roll was surrounded by country music, which is clear in his songs. His Nashville roots are especially strong in his storytelling style, where he often talks about life's struggles and triumphs, just like traditional country music.

Southern Musical Elements: Jelly Roll includes many Southern music elements in his songs, such as the use of guitars, banjos, and harmonicas. His lyrics often reflect themes of Southern life, including the importance of family, faith, and overcoming hardships.

Southern Storytelling in His Lyrics: A big part of Southern music is telling stories, and Jelly Roll does this in his songs. He shares personal stories about his life, including his challenges with addiction and his journey to becoming a better person. This storytelling helps him connect with listeners.

Influence of Southern Artists: Jelly Roll has mentioned being inspired by Southern musicians like Johnny Cash, who also sang about personal struggles. He blends these influences with his love for hip-hop and rock, creating a style that's both Southern and modern.

Balancing Southern and Contemporary Elements: While Jelly Roll includes many Southern influences in his music, he also blends them with more urban and contemporary sounds, like rap beats and modern production techniques. This balance makes his music feel both classic and fresh at the same time.

Impact on Southern Music: Jelly Roll's music both honors Southern traditions and challenges them. By mixing hip-hop and rock with country, he pushes the boundaries of what Southern music can be. His unique style adds something new to the Southern music landscape.

Cultural Background and Genre Blending: Jelly Roll's background growing up in the South and his experiences in life influence how he approaches different genres. His ability to mix different types of music reflects his diverse upbringing and makes his sound stand out in today's music world.

Chapter 7: Achievements

Chart Success and Awards:

Notable Songs on Music Charts: Jelly Roll has had several songs that reached important spots on music charts. For example, his song "Son of a Sinner" did very well on the Billboard Country Airplay chart, climbing high into the top 10. Another song, "Save Me," gained a lot of attention and performed strongly across multiple charts, including rock and country.

Number-One Hits and Top 10 Performances: While Jelly Roll has not always hit number one, he's had songs reach the top 10 on important charts. "Son of a Sinner" was a breakthrough hit, staying on the chart for many weeks, showing how well his music connects with fans.

Album Performance on Charts: Jelly Roll's albums have also made an impact on album charts. His album Ballads of the Broken climbed the Billboard 200 chart, which tracks the most popular albums in the U.S. It also did well on other charts, like Top Country Albums and Top Rock Albums, showing his ability to reach fans across different genres.

Gold and Platinum Certifications: Several of Jelly Roll's songs have been awarded gold or platinum certifications. This means they've sold a large number of copies. For example, "Save Me" has achieved gold status, proving it's a fan favorite with over 500,000 sales.

Major Music Awards: Jelly Roll has won several music awards that highlight his talent. He won at the CMT Music Awards, which honors country music videos and performances. He's also been nominated for other major awards, like the iHeartRadio Music Awards, which shows how far he's come in the music world.

Impact on His Career: These chart successes and awards have helped Jelly Roll grow in his career. As his songs climb higher on the charts and he wins more awards, he gains more fans and recognition. These achievements have opened doors for him, including bigger tours and more opportunities to collaborate with other artists.

Comparison Across Genres: Jelly Roll's chart success shows that he doesn't fit into just one genre. His songs perform well on country, hip-hop, and rock charts, which is rare for many artists. This proves that his music appeals to a wide audience.

Turning Points in His Career: Jelly Roll's career has taken off in recent years. "Son of a Sinner" was a major turning point, helping him gain more attention. As he releases more music, his success continues to grow, showing that his hard work is paying off.

Social Media and Streaming Milestones

Follower Counts on Social Media: Jelly Roll has a strong social media presence. He has millions of followers on platforms like Instagram, Twitter, and TikTok. His Instagram alone has over 2 million followers, where he regularly shares updates and personal stories.

Viral Moments and Social Media Success: One of Jelly Roll's viral moments was when he shared a heartfelt video talking about his journey through addiction. This post touched many people and was shared widely, helping him gain even more followers. His TikTok videos also regularly get millions of views, showcasing his funny and real personality.

Fan Engagement on Social Media: Jelly Roll stays connected with his fans through social media. He often replies to comments, shares fan posts, and talks openly about his struggles. This helps him build a loyal fanbase that feels personally connected to him. His down-to-earth style makes people feel like they know him.

Streaming Milestones: On streaming platforms like Spotify, Jelly Roll's songs have racked up millions of plays. "Save Me" alone has over 100 million streams on Spotify, and his total career streams are in the hundreds of millions. His songs are featured on popular playlists, which helps more people discover his music.

Playlisting Achievements: Jelly Roll's music appears on some of Spotify's biggest playlists, like New Music Friday and Hot Country. These playlists introduce his music to new listeners and help boost his streaming numbers.

Notable Streaming Achievements: Jelly Roll has achieved impressive streaming records for someone who crosses genres. His songs are among the most streamed in both the country and rock categories, showing that his mix of styles resonates with fans across different music tastes.

Connection Between Streaming and Chart Success: Jelly Roll's strong streaming numbers help push his songs up the charts. As more people stream his music, it gets more attention from radio stations and media outlets, which leads to even more success.

How He Uses Social Media and Streaming: Jelly Roll uses platforms like YouTube, Spotify, and Instagram to connect with fans and share new music. He often posts sneak peeks of new songs or behind-the-scenes footage from his tours. This keeps fans excited and engaged, helping him promote his music without needing traditional advertising.

Comparison to Other Artists: Jelly Roll's digital presence is impressive when compared to other artists in his genres. He has more social media followers and higher streaming numbers than many artists who stick to one genre. His ability to connect with fans online is a big reason for his success.

Reflecting Changes in Music Trends: Jelly Roll's success on social media and streaming platforms reflects how much the music industry has changed. In today's world, artists need to connect with fans online, and Jelly Roll has mastered this. His achievements show that having a strong digital presence is just as important as making good music.

Chapter 8: Philanthropy and Advocacy

Mental Health Advocacy and Public Speaking

Openness About Mental Health: Jelly Roll has always been open about his struggles with mental health. He talks honestly about his experiences with depression and anxiety, which has helped many of his fans feel less alone. His honesty encourages others to speak up about their own problems, and this openness has created a strong bond with his audience.

Speaking Engagements and Interviews: Jelly Roll has given many interviews and speeches where he talks about mental health. He has appeared on podcasts and radio shows, sharing his personal journey. His words have made a big impact because people can relate to what he's been through.

Involvement in Mental Health Awareness: Jelly Roll is active in raising awareness about mental health. He's been part of campaigns that encourage people to seek help when they're struggling. His voice in these conversations is important because he's seen as someone who understands what it's like to face tough mental health challenges.

Mental Health Themes in His Music: Mental health is a key theme in many of Jelly Roll's songs. He writes about feeling broken, lost, and trying to heal. His music often touches on the pain of depression but also offers hope and resilience, which resonates with his fans and helps start important conversations about mental wellness.

Partnerships with Mental Health Organizations: Jelly Roll has teamed up with mental health organizations to spread awareness and provide support for those who need it. These partnerships help get important messages out to more people, using his platform to make a real difference.

Impact on Reducing Stigma: Through his music and his public talks, Jelly Roll has helped reduce the stigma around mental health. He's shown that it's okay to struggle and that asking for help is a sign of strength. This has been especially meaningful in the music industry, where mental health isn't always talked about openly.

Personal Experiences Informing Advocacy: Jelly Roll's own life experiences are at the heart of his advocacy. Having been through tough times himself, he knows how important it is to speak up about mental health. His fans trust him because he's lived through many of the issues he talks about.

Promoting Mental Health Resources: Jelly Roll often encourages his fans to seek out therapy, support groups, and other resources if they're struggling. He knows how important it is to have a strong support system and often shares tips on how to cope with difficult emotions.

Evolution of His Advocacy Work: As Jelly Roll's career has grown, so has his work in mental health advocacy. He continues to find new ways to talk about mental wellness and reach more people, whether through his music, social media, or public speaking.

Charity Work and Community Outreach

Charities and Causes He Supports: Jelly Roll is passionate about giving back to those in need, especially when it comes to addiction recovery and helping at-risk youth. He has supported charities that work with people struggling with addiction and has also focused on causes related to criminal justice reform. These are important to him because of his own past experiences.

Benefit Concerts and Events: Jelly Roll has been part of many benefit concerts that raise money for important causes. Whether he's performing to help a local charity or raising awareness about addiction, his concerts have made a real impact on the people who need it most.

Work with Local Communities: Jelly Roll is very active in his hometown of Nashville. He often gives back to the community by supporting programs that help people turn their lives around. This includes mentoring young people and working with organizations that help those who've been through tough times.

Donations and Fundraising Efforts: Jelly Roll has made donations to several charities and has helped raise money through special events. His generosity has been felt by many, especially in causes related to addiction and helping people in recovery. He believes in giving others the same chance at a better life that he got.

Personal Experiences Influencing His Charity Work: Jelly Roll's difficult past is what drives his charity work. Having faced addiction and other challenges himself, he's committed to helping others who are in similar situations. He understands their struggles and wants to make a difference in their lives.

Programs to Help Aspiring Musicians: Jelly Roll has also supported programs that help aspiring musicians. He knows how hard it can be to break into the music industry, so he tries to give back by offering support to young artists. He's particularly interested in helping those who come from tough backgrounds, just like he did.

Impact of His Charitable Work: Jelly Roll's charity work has made a huge difference, both for the people who benefit from it and for his public image. Fans respect him not just for his music, but for his heart and his dedication to helping others.

Recognition for His Philanthropy: Jelly Roll has been recognized for his charity efforts. While awards and recognition aren't his main goal, people have noticed the good he's doing, and it has earned him even more respect in both the music and charitable communities.

Balancing Charity and Music Career: Balancing his charity work with his music career and personal life can be challenging, but Jelly Roll is committed to both. He makes time for the causes he believes in, even when he's busy touring or working on new music. This balance reflects the themes in his songs about overcoming challenges and giving back to those who need it.

Charity Reflecting His Music Themes: Jelly Roll's charity work mirrors the themes in his music. Just like his songs talk about overcoming addiction and finding strength, his charitable efforts focus on helping others through those same struggles. His real-life actions match the messages in his music, making his outreach even more powerful.

Chapter 9: Challenges and Controversies

Legal Troubles:

Jelly Roll (Jason DeFord) has been candid about his troubled past, particularly his involvement with the law, which has significantly influenced both his personal life and music career. His legal troubles began in his teenage years, with a series of arrests related to drug offenses. He was first arrested as a minor, and his involvement in selling drugs led to additional charges as he grew older. One of his most notable arrests took place in Nashville, Tennessee, where he was charged with drug distribution. His repeated run-ins with the law ultimately resulted in time spent in juvenile detention centers, followed by a more extended stint in prison.

These experiences with the criminal justice system left a lasting impact on Jelly Roll. During his time in prison, he began to reflect on the direction of his life and decided to pursue music as a way to turn things around. His time behind bars fueled much of his songwriting, with lyrics that delve into the harsh realities of addiction, crime, and the desire for redemption. In public interviews, he has been open about his legal history, often using it as a platform to speak about the importance of second chances and personal growth.

Although his criminal record initially posed challenges, such as difficulties securing gigs and being restricted from performing in certain venues, Jelly Roll has managed to rebuild his life. His openness about his past has earned him a loyal fanbase, many of whom relate to his struggles. Additionally, he has used his platform to advocate for criminal justice reform, encouraging people to avoid the mistakes he made and offering support to those seeking a fresh start. His advocacy work, coupled with his transparency about his legal issues, has strengthened his relationship with fans and shown the music industry that he is committed to personal growth.

Criticisms and Industry Setbacks:

Despite his success, Jelly Roll has faced his share of challenges and criticisms in the music industry. Early in his career, he struggled to gain mainstream recognition due to his unconventional blend of hip-hop, country, and rock. Many industry professionals were unsure how to market his unique style, and genre purists in both hip-hop and country were skeptical of his ability to authentically represent their musical traditions. Critics often pointed to his genre-blending approach as a weakness, questioning whether he could be taken seriously in any one style of music.

Another hurdle for Jelly Roll was gaining radio play. His lyrics, which frequently touch on raw themes like addiction and crime, were seen as too gritty or controversial for mainstream radio stations. Furthermore, his heavily tattooed appearance and troubled background likely

...he industry perceived him, creating additional barriers influenced by more conservative music circles to accept...

...career setbacks, Jelly Roll has experienced challenges with ...s that didn't pan out and projects that were poorly received. ...his portrayal of addiction and recovery in his music has ...criticism, with some suggesting that his songs might ...icize the darker aspects of his past. He has also faced obstacles ...aking through to mainstream music awards and industry events, ...en being overlooked due to his background and outsider status.

Despite these challenges, Jelly Roll has used criticism as fuel for his career. He has remained steadfast in his commitment to making authentic music, regardless of industry expectations, and his ability to connect with fans has helped him overcome many of the setbacks he's faced. Today, his genre-blending style is widely celebrated, and his openness about his personal struggles continues to resonate deeply with his audience. Through persistence, Jelly Roll has turned many of the criticisms and setbacks into opportunities for growth, proving that staying true to himself was the key to his long-term success.

Chapter 10: Legacy and Future

Influence on Music and Upcoming Projects

Jelly Roll's lasting impact on the music industry stems largely from his ability to blend genres like hip-hop, country, and rock in a way that feels authentic and emotionally raw. His cross-genre success has influenced other artists who now feel more comfortable experimenting with different musical styles, especially in country and rock, where tradition often rules. By staying true to his roots and telling personal, often painful stories, Jelly Roll has opened doors for a new wave of musicians who want to blend modern and traditional sounds while delivering genuine, heartfelt lyrics.

In mainstream country and rock, Jelly Roll is seen as a key figure in making room for more gritty, real-life storytelling, which has been embraced by fans seeking deeper connections with the music. His influence can be seen in younger artists who are following his lead, mixing genres while maintaining a focus on authenticity.

Looking ahead, Jelly Roll has hinted at several exciting projects. Fans eagerly await his upcoming album releases, which promise to explore new musical directions while staying true to his signature sound. His tours are always in demand, drawing huge crowds, and his future performances will likely continue to showcase his evolution as an artist. Additionally, Jelly Roll has expressed interest in expanding his brand beyond music, perhaps exploring business ventures, merchandise, and other creative endeavors.

Industry experts predict continued success for Jelly Roll, with many believing that his legacy will be one of bridging genres and breaking down barriers for artists with unconventional backgrounds. He's already inspiring a new generation of musicians who come from difficult circumstances, showing that it's possible to rise above personal challenges and make a meaningful impact in the music industry.

Impact on Southern Hip-Hop and Country Rap

Jelly Roll has played a significant role in shaping the evolution of Southern hip-hop and country rap. His unique style has helped push these genres forward by bringing together elements of traditional country music with the rhythm and storytelling of hip-hop. This fusion has contributed to the growing popularity of country rap, a genre that blends rural themes and modern rap beats.

As an artist deeply rooted in the South, Jelly Roll has successfully bridged the gap between country and hip-hop audiences, offering a sound that speaks to fans of both genres. His Southern roots shine through in his music, where he frequently references his experiences growing up in Nashville and the struggles he's faced along the way.

Jelly Roll's approach can be compared to other notable figures in country rap, like Bubba Sparxxx or Colt Ford, but his music tends to lean more heavily on personal storytelling. This has earned him praise for bringing a new level of depth to the genre, legitimizing country rap in the eyes of many mainstream country listeners. His collaborations with other Southern hip-hop and country rap artists have helped further solidify his role in the genre's development.

Criticism from purists in both country and hip-hop circles has been inevitable, as some see his blending of genres as straying too far from tradition. However, Jelly Roll has largely overcome this by staying true to his experiences and using his platform to bring attention to the themes of addiction, recovery, and personal growth, which resonate with a broad audience.

Overall, Jelly Roll's contributions to Southern hip-hop and country rap have not only expanded the genres but also opened doors for similar artists who are looking to blend musical styles while staying true to their roots.

Chapter 11: Discography

Albums, Mixtapes, and Key Singles

Jelly Roll has an extensive catalog of music that reflects his journey from underground artist to mainstream success. Here's a breakdown of his key releases:

Studio Albums:

Each of Jelly Roll's studio albums showcases his growth as an artist. Some of his most notable albums include A Beautiful Disaster (2020) and Ballads of the Broken (2021), both of which climbed various charts and gained significant attention. The latter debuted on Billboard's Top Rock Albums, highlighting his crossover appeal. These albums reflect his evolution from raw, rap-heavy tracks to more polished blends of country, rock, and hip-hop.

Mixtapes and Independent Releases:

Early in his career, Jelly Roll built his fanbase through numerous independent releases and mixtapes. His Therapeutic Music series is particularly notable for addressing his personal struggles with addiction and mental health, connecting deeply with his audience. These mixtapes established him as an artist unafraid to dive into deeply personal themes, long before mainstream success.

Key Singles:

Jelly Roll's hit singles like "Save Me" and "Son of a Sinner" have been career-defining. "Save Me" became a viral sensation and showcases his vulnerable side, blending heartfelt lyrics with a soulful melody. "Son of a Sinner," from Ballads of the Broken, became a crossover hit, reaching high positions on both the country and rock charts. These singles not only earned him more fans but also proved his ability to create deeply emotional, resonant songs that transcend genre boundaries.

Evolution of Sound:

Throughout his career, Jelly Roll has evolved from a primarily rap artist to a genre-blending force. Early releases were rap-heavy, but over time, he incorporated more elements of rock and country, reflecting both his Southern roots and personal growth. His lyrics have also shifted from gritty, street-focused storytelling to deeper reflections on life, addiction, recovery, and resilience.

Critical Reception:

His major releases have received a mix of critical praise, particularly for their emotional honesty and raw storytelling. Critics often note his ability to bring depth to the country-rap hybrid genre, and while some purists may be skeptical of his genre-blending approach, his fanbase continues to grow.

Significant Tracks:

Some of Jelly Roll's most impactful songs include "Save Me," "Bottle and Mary Jane," and "Creature." These tracks delve into his personal battles, offering a raw and unfiltered view of his life experiences. They also highlight his versatility as both a rapper and singer, capable of delivering gut-wrenching emotion through his vocals.

Collaborations:

Over the years, Jelly Roll has collaborated with a wide range of artists, from fellow country-rap figures like Struggle Jennings to rock acts like Tech N9ne. These collaborations further showcase his ability to blend genres and appeal to diverse audiences.

His personal experiences with addiction, incarceration, and recovery are evident in every release, making his discography a true reflection of his life's highs and lows. Each album marks a different stage in his career, with earlier works focused on survival and hustle, and later albums reflecting a more introspective, emotionally complex artist navigating fame and redemption.

Music Videos and Visual Projects:

Jelly Roll has also used music videos and other visual media to amplify his storytelling and connect more deeply with fans. His visual artistry plays a significant role in his overall appeal.

Key Music Videos:

Some of Jelly Roll's most significant music videos include "Save Me" and "Creature." The video for "Save Me," directed by Patrick Tohill, is a stark, intimate portrayal of Jelly Roll's emotional pain, shot simply in black and white. This raw approach enhances the song's emotional depth and has resonated with millions of viewers, helping the track go viral. "Creature" showcases a darker, more intense side, with visuals that reflect the song's themes of inner demons and struggles with addiction.

Visual Themes:

Over time, Jelly Roll's music videos have become more polished and conceptual, often reflecting the themes of his music, such as addiction, recovery, and personal growth. Early videos were often gritty and raw, mirroring his underground roots, but as his career has progressed, his videos have become more cinematic and visually striking.

Awards and Recognition:

While his music videos haven't received significant awards recognition, they have garnered millions of views on platforms like YouTube, further cementing his connection with his fanbase. The emotional impact of his videos, particularly those for his more introspective songs, continues to draw praise from fans and critics alike.

Visual Storytelling and Personality:

Jelly Roll uses visual media to tell his story in a way that words alone cannot. His tattoos, rugged appearance, and soulful eyes are integral to his persona, and this comes through clearly in his music videos. Fans connect not only with the words he sings but with the vulnerability and authenticity he conveys visually.

Documentaries and Concert Films:

Jelly Roll has been involved in a few visual projects beyond music videos, including concert films that showcase his energy and connection with audiences. His openness about his personal struggles often shines through in these live performances, where he speaks candidly between songs.

Innovative Approaches:

Jelly Roll has also embraced social media as part of his visual storytelling. Platforms like Instagram and TikTok allow him to share more intimate, behind-the-scenes content with his fans. This constant engagement helps build a deeper connection, making his fans feel like they are part of his journey.

Social Media and Music Videos:

His presence on platforms like YouTube, Instagram, and TikTok plays a huge role in his ability to connect visually with his audience.

Short-form video content, whether clips from his daily life or snippets from music video shoots, keeps his fans engaged and builds anticipation for new releases.

Chapter 12: Fan Base and Influence

Interaction with Fans

Jelly Roll has a personal relationship with his fans, marked by his honesty and ongoing interaction.

Fan Engagement and Accessibility:

He interacts with fans through social media, sharing behind-the-scenes moments and responding to comments, making him relatable.

Unique Connections:

He organizes meet-and-greet events and offers personal experiences at concerts, allowing fans to feel more connected.

Impact of Authenticity:

His openness about addiction, mental health, and his past has earned him loyal fans, many of whom relate to his struggles.

Fan Reactions:

Fans often share how his music helps them through tough times, creating a strong emotional connection.

Charitable Initiatives with Fans:

Jelly Roll involves his fans in charity work, like raising awareness for addiction recovery, fostering a sense of community.

Balancing Fame with Connection:

Despite growing fame, he stays grounded by making his audience feel appreciated.

Notable Fan Stories:

Fans often tell stories of how Jelly Roll's music has made a difference in their lives, showing his deep influence.

Influence on Emerging Artists

Jelly Roll's success has inspired many up-and-coming musicians, especially those with unconventional backgrounds.

Mentoring New Artists:

He mentors and collaborates with new artists, sharing their work with his fans.

Opening Doors for Unconventional Artists:

His mix of country, rock, and hip-hop has shown others that success is possible without fitting into one category.

Collaborations with New Talent:

Jelly Roll frequently works with emerging artists, helping them gain exposure.

Inspiration for Artists from Similar Backgrounds:

His journey from a troubled past to success motivates aspiring musicians with similar struggles.

Influence on New Music Trends:

His genre-blending style has influenced new music trends and opened doors for other artists.

Changing Industry Perceptions:

Jelly Roll has changed how the music industry views artists with difficult pasts, showing they can still succeed.

Social Media Presence

Jelly Roll uses social media to promote his music and stay connected with fans.

Content Creation Across Platforms:

He shares personal moments on Instagram, fun videos on TikTok, and communicates directly with fans on Twitter.

Music Promotion and Fan Connection:

He balances promoting his music with personal posts, keeping his fans engaged.

Viral Moments:

His candid and unfiltered content has gone viral, spreading his music to new audiences.

Reflection of Personality and Brand:

His social media reflects his music's themes of honesty and resilience, strengthening his personal brand.

www.ingramcontent.com/pod-product-compliance
Lightning Source LLC
LaVergne TN
LVHW021616231224
799802LV00035B/1167